MIX
Papier aus verantwortungsvollen Quellen
Paper from responsible sources
FSC® C105338

Dr. Tan Kwan Hong

ASEAN's Energy Architecture

An In-Depth Analysis and Forecast on ASEAN's Energy Supply and Demand Balances

Anchor Academic Publishing

Executive Summary

The lack of access to electricity constitutes a major challenge faced by millions of rural households in the region. The region also faces a steep surge of demand for in the next two decades, so much so that despite having a considerable amount of coal and gas in the region, more will still need to be imported. The usage of oil and coal will remain as the dominant source of energy till 2030, and will continue to contribute to global warming.

The evaluation of nuclear power as an energy option is a top research focus of several ASEAN countries, and will be discussed and analyzed in this paper. And although the push for renewable energy have been spearheaded throughout ASEAN, renewable energy sources will contribute to only a small portion of overall energy requirements of the region, and will remain at best, a supplementary energy source.

Apart from electricity production, ASEAN will witness a phenomenal increase in vehicle ownership over the next two decades, resulting in staggering demand for gasoline and diesel, of which most of it has to be imported. Adopting bio-fuels as a substitute transport fuel is touted to be slow and controversial.

Mega ASEAN initiatives such as the regional power and gas pipeline networks are remarkable intentions, but progress on a regional level has been slow. Finally, energy efficiency and local energy problems faced by individual countries are causes for concern. These national issues will affect how energy cooperation will pan out on a regional level.

Chapter 1: ASEAN Energy Supply and Demand Balance Analysis

Energy remains the vital enabler that allows countries to provide key essentials – food, water, education, health care and national security – to their citizens. A fully functioning society thus requires an abundant and affordable supply of energy to sustain urbanization, modernization and development.

Despite its crucial importance, stunning insights emerge from current supply and demand Balance. First, electrification rates in ASEAN remained stunningly low. ASEAN, with a population of 567 million people, comprises of a startling proportion of 160.3 million people who do not have access to electricity, using twigs and leaves to cook their food. Electrification rates vary widely throughout the ASEAN region, ranging from 10% in Myanmar to 100% in Singapore (Exhibit 1). With a projected GDP growth rate that is expected to supersede that of the world and of advanced economies till 2016 (Exhibit 2), ASEAN is expected to increase its reliance on coal (Exhibit 3), and reduce its reliance on oil (Exhibit 3) till 2030. Additionally, energy derived from biomass and waste will grow by more than 10% per annum (Exhibit 4). However, despite these growth rates, growth in total final energy consumption is expected to stabilize beyond 2015 (Exhibit 5), resulting in a major reliance on coal and gas by 2030 (Exhibit 6).

The energy resource types utilized by different ASEAN member countries vary widely (Exhibit 7). Despite so, the region's reliance on Oil and Gas as a total share of energy demand is likely to remain constant from 2020 to 2030 (Exhibit 8). ASEAN's dealings with nuclear energy remained insignificant in 2009 (Exhibit 9), and will remain so till 2030 (Exhibit 8).

Chapter 2: Electricity Generation in ASEAN

ASEAN relies heavily on coal to generate electricity (Exhibit 10), and this reliance on coal is expected to rise over the next decade. Coal is currently still the most affordable and convenient fuel to satisfy the expected rise in electricity demand. However, the environment will be compromised. The burning of coal releases more carbon dioxide per unit of energy than oil and natural gas. The lifecycle of coal – from mining, transportation and burning of coal – leads to major environmental and health hazards, from smog and acid rain production, to mercury pollution in rivers, and even to asthma and other respiratory ailments.

The region will increase its reliance on natural gas for electricity production over the next decade. Singapore and Thailand currently imports large quantities of natural gas, while Malaysia, Brunei and Myanmar all exports it (Exhibit 11). According to forecasts done by the International Energy Agency (IEA), unconventional natural gas will provide for 40% of the increase in global energy supply. IEA also estimates that total recoverable conventional gas resources can support 120 years of current consumption globally. Natural gas is also more environmentally friendly than coal.

The ASEAN region will also rely less on oil for electricity generation over the next decade. Oil is the most expensive method of electricity production, and highly polluting. It is thus wiser to refine the oil and utilize these petroleum products in the transport sector. Cambodia currently depends heavily on oil for electricity generation via diesel generators because it has yet to utilize coal or oil powered plants (Exhibit 10).

Finally, when electricity generation is concerned, nuclear power plants remained a questionable alternative. Nuclear power does not contribute to global warming and climate changes, and can be a potential energy source as ASEAN currently lacks adequate domestic coal, gas and oil. Also, many ASEAN governments are currently subsidizing the cost of electricity and thus bear the burden of volatile fossil fuel import prices, and nuclear energy could be a way out of this predicament. However, nuclear power plants simultaneously poses a series of concerns – high cost to develop, long lead time for construction of these plants, a lack of skilled technicians, difficulties in disposal of nuclear wastes, and need for constant maintenance. Terrorist attacks on these plants or during the transportation of radioactive materials are real issues, along with theft of radioactive or nuclear materials that could potentially occur. Incidents at these plants or during the transport of radioactive materials could release undesirable amounts of radioactive materials to the environment.

As of the post-Fukushima era, Vietnam will continue on its plans to construct nuclear power plants. Agreements with Russia and Japan to build two 1000 MY reactors has been firmed up. Russia will embark on building the first plant in 2013. Indonesia, Malaysia, Singapore and the Philippines all continued studies on this option. Only Thailand has placed its nuclear projects on hold.

Chapter 3: Transport Fuel Utilization in ASEAN

The transport sectors of Indonesia, Malaysia, Singapore, Thailand, Vietnam and the Philippines accounted for 17-35% of total energy consumption in 2009 (Exhibit 12). Transport consumption is positively correlated to economic growth, and vehicle population for several ASEAN countries (Indonesia, Malaysia, Singapore, Thailand, Vietnam and the Philippines) combined are expected to grow from 10 million vehicles in 1990, to 79 million in 2030 (Exhibit 13). The projected transport sector consumption of energy of these same countries combined is estimated to rise from 87 Mtoe in 2007 to 176 Mtoe in 2020, and to 299 Mtoe in 2030 (Exhibit 14). Correspondingly, the share of energy due to transport consumption is estimated to rise from 24.6% in 2007 to 29.2% by 2020, and will rise marginally once more to 31% in 2030 (Exhibit 14). In per capita terms, this translates to a surge from 26 vehicles per 1000 persons in 2010, to 127 vehicles per 1000 persons in 2030, a massive 492% increase (Exhibit 15)!

Chapter 4: Heavy Reliance on Petroleum Product Imports

Apart from the growing energy demands from transport that ASEAN has to cope with, ASEAN's reliance on petroleum product imports sees a rising trend. Around 1999, ASEAN went from being a net exporter to a net importer of petroleum products (Exhibit 16). And among all ASEAN countries, Cambodia and Laos have to import all their required refined products due to the non-existence of refineries in their country (Exhibit 17). Thus, these countries are most exposed to price volatilities of refined products, and energy security due to refined products remains a concern.

Chapter 5: Fuel Subsidies A Major Problem

The provision of fuel subsidies by some ASEAN countries (Malaysia and Indonesia have the highest expenditures on fuel subsidies, while the Philippines and Thailand provide targeted subsidies for public transport) (Exhibit 18) might reduce the government's fiscal budget needed to fund alternative development programmes, especially those targeted towards the lower income group. Fuel subsidies also create a strain on government budgets, particularly in times of high fuel prices. These subsidies also distort economic prices, discourage energy efficiency improvements and promote wasteful consumption.

Additionally, inequality in subsidies might also exist. In Indonesia, high income families benefit the most, as 40% of these high income families benefit from 70% of the fuel subsidies, while 40% of the lowest income families benefit from 15% of the subsidies. In 2011, fuel subsidies eroded about $14 billion or 11% of Indonesia's state budget, far exceeding the $2.3 billion devoted to education and health combined.

Singapore is the only ASEAN country to dispense with fuel subsidies. However, diesel and gasoline prices are most expensive out of all ASEAN countries (Exhibits 18 and 19).

Chapter 6: Ending Fuel Subsidies

Although many ASEAN countries have had intentions to reduce or eradicate fuel subsidies due to high oil prices that had put a strain on government expenditure, it has been difficult to do so without arousing public objection. For example, in 1998, a rise in fuel prices in Indonesia sparked off student-led riots, which ended President Suharto's 32-year presidentship.

Ten years later, in 2008, an oil subsidy cut in Malaysia triggered student protests, of which resulted in the ruling coalition losing a third of its parliamentary seats and control of five states to the opposition.

More recently, in April 2012, weeks of protests forced the Indonesian government to overturn plans calling for an immediate surge in fuel prices.

Chapter 7: Strategies to End Fuel Subsidies

Grasping the right timing to remove fuel subsidies is key when it comes to minimizing the impact of political fallout. In April 2012, the Taiwanese government, upon foreseeing no major elections coming up for the next four years, took advantage of that timing to eradicate fuel subsidies and raise petrol prices by 10%. Moments of relatively low oil prices could also constitute golden opportunities in the removal of fuel subsidies. In 2009, oil prices were at around $35 per barrel, compared to over $100 per barrel today.

Chapter 8: Regional Power and Gas Pipeline Networks

Energy was identified as a key area of cooperation since the founding of ASEAN in 1967. Initially, cooperation was perceived as the best way of enhancing energy security. However, in recent years, the role of environment on this process is increasing seen as vital. These principles were significant in shaping ASEAN's approach to energy security. In 1997, the Heads of State at the Second ASEAN Informal Summit in Kuala Lumpur envisioned an energy-integrated ASEAN, to be spearheaded by two ambitious projects:

1. The ASEAN Power Grid Project (APG) (Exhibit 20)
2. The Trans-ASEAN Gas Pipeline (TAGP) (Exhibit 21)

Chapter 9: Slow Progress on the APG and TAGP

However, progress on such projects on a mega-scale has been slow, and is expected to remain slow going forward, given the complexity and scale of the task. For the APG, existing grid connections have been mainly driven by bilateral arrangements, signifying that full-fledge electricity trading on an ASEAN level might not materialize in the near term.

Furthermore, progress on the TAGP did not turn out as expected, as most developments achieved to date are on bilateral arrangements. Transformations in the natural gas market coupled with technological advancements have caused impediments to the expansions of the TAGP and its development plan as previously envisioned. Finally, the flexibility of transporting and storing Liquefied Natural Gas (LNG), a substitute to pipeline transportation of gas, would most likely win over governments in the region.

Chapter 10: The Potential Role of Renewable Energy

While energy cooperation might be an uphill task due to both the increasing demand pressures for energy consumption and to the numerous challenges expounded upon throughout this article, a silver lining exist for an environmentally-friendly ASEAN: Several major ASEAN countries have pledged to reduce carbon emissions and energy intensity (Exhibit 22). Of which,

Indonesia has shown the greatest potential for adopting renewable energy sources by 2030 (Exhibit 23). Indonesia and the Philippines will possess large geothermal reserves.

However, despite the large potential of renewable energy sources, wind, solar, geothermal and hydropower sources of energy can at best, play a supplementary role to fossil fuels, as the latter will remain the undisputed primary energy source for ASEAN.

The demand for bio-fuels is also expected to soar in meeting the increasing demand for private vehicles. Additionally, the decline in the region's oil reserve, and the huge reliance on oil imports that result in worsening trade balances and an outflow of foreign exchange reserves are divers in increasing bio-fuel demands in the region.

If this pans out well, countries will reduce their risks and exposure to the rising prices of oil, and governments can even reduce oil subsidization to improve their fiscal position over the long run. The development of the bio-fuel industry to meet the soaring demand can also potentially lift thousands of rural residents out of poverty.

Current, ASEAN's major bio-fuel produces are Indonesia, Malaysia, Thailand and the Philippines (Exhibit 9), and will likely remain so.

Despite the large potential for bio-fuels as an energy source, governments will need to mitigate the side effects that come with its usage. Deforestation, soil and water depletion, loss of biodiversity and farmland, eutrophication and haze are all potential risks. The potential reduction of overall carbon dioxide emissions is also questionable, given the high-energy consumption of bio-fuels. Further, the first generation of bio-fuels is food crops. Increasing demand for these crops can put undesired pressure on oil prices and even exacerbate poverty.

Chapter 11: The Fifth Fuel: Energy Efficiency

Finally, enhancing energy efficiency is an often-overlooked factor in ASEAN energy policy developments. Several ASEAN countries face high transmission and distribution losses of electricity (Exhibit 24). This adds on to wasted resources, and to the cost of energy production.

ASEAN must therefore convey the right message that emphasizes how energy efficiency can contribute to economic growth, diverting more attention to such important issues apart from climate change mitigation. Countries will also need scale up energy efficiency via technological improvements and adopt energy-saving best practices. A two-pronged strategy of regulatory best practices and financial incentives are needed to promote energy efficient market transformations, and their exact composition will vary from country to country. Governments could also tap into carbon financing as a major financial incentive to help scale up energy efficiency in markets.

Chapter 12: Conclusion and Outlook

Before large scale ASEAN energy initiatives can be implemented successfully, it is recommended that countries have their respective challenges fixed on the national level first and foremost, before the benefits of regional cooperation can be materialized. ASEAN countries face vastly different national energy challenges, from improving rural electrification in Myanmar to reducing energy subsidies in Malaysia and Indonesia (Exhibit 25). The success of major programmes adopted by individual countries towards improving access to electricity is vital (Exhibit 26). Thus, policies, programmes and challenges on a national level will affect multilateral energy cooperation on a regional platform.

To build momentum for future energy projects on a mega scale, ASEAN can start by leveraging on each country's common goal for environmental well-being and carbon emission reduction. This will get countries to start of at the same page so as to build momentum for deeper cooperation in subsequent meetings.

Countries should also jointly recognize price volatilities of current major sources of energy, as well as the increasing demand for energy in the next decade. Such a common recognition will help to better facilitate closer cooperation towards the diversification of energy sources, sharing of expertise for enhancing energy efficiency, and for creating a joint energy pool. The co-development of new energy technologies for efficient energy production is also another commonly overlooked avenue for cooperation that has scope for improvements.

Beyond the realm of energy policy-making, helping to expedite the development and urbanization of underdeveloped countries, especially Myanmar, will be an imperative for the successful implementation of future ASEAN energy policies. Having member countries that are more urbanized and developed can lead to more regional economic and trade benefits, for example, by raising intra-regional trade through increased import consumption due to increased income. Any hopes for an ASEAN joint energy market where energy can be traded through an integrated platform, and where financial instruments can be utilized for risk mitigation, risk transfer, hedging and transactional purposes, can thus be build upon this foundation.

The private sector operating in the energy sector also has a major role to play. Increasingly, these businesses will have to shift from a pre-dominantly localized mindset into a more regionalized mindset. For example, cooperate development strategies and market segmentation strategies will increasingly have to bear into consideration the ASEAN customer base (not just the local customer base), ASEAN stakeholders, rules and regulations of ASEAN countries etc. Have a regionalized mindset that is acutely aware of the specific energy needs of individual markets will allow companies to adapt to the increasingly integrated ASEAN energy market in the next two decades.

Finally, ASEAN needs to recognize that the most favorable time for energy cooperation is NOW. Opportunities presented due to technological developments and new energy best practices are aplenty. The region also has the potential to "leapfrog" to the newest energy technologies, and not go through the inefficient and environmentally degrading industrial and energy revolutions that the rest of the world went through. Fostering a greater energy interdependence will also lead to greater economic and security interdependence, thus paving the way for more intimate joint cooperation via an enlightened leadership in the future.

Exhibits

Exhibit 1: Electrification Rates of ASEAN Countries

Country	Electrification Rate (%)			Millions
	Total	Urban	Rural	Population without electricity
Brunei	99.7	100.0	98.6	0.0
Cambodia	24.0	66.0	12.5	11.2
Indonesia	64.5	94.0	32.0	81.1
Laos	55.0	84.0	42.0	2.7
Malaysia	99.4	100.0	98.0	0.2
Myanmar	13.0	19.0	10.0	42.8
Philippines	86.0	97.0	65.0	12.5
Singapore	100.0	100.0	100.0	0.0
Thailand	99.3	100.0	99.0	0.4
Vietnam	89.0	99.6	85.0	9.5
ASEAN Region	71.9	91.3	54.9	160.3

Source: International Energy Agency Electricity Access Database

Exhibit 2: ASEAN, World and Advanced Economies. Projected GDP Growth Rate till 2016

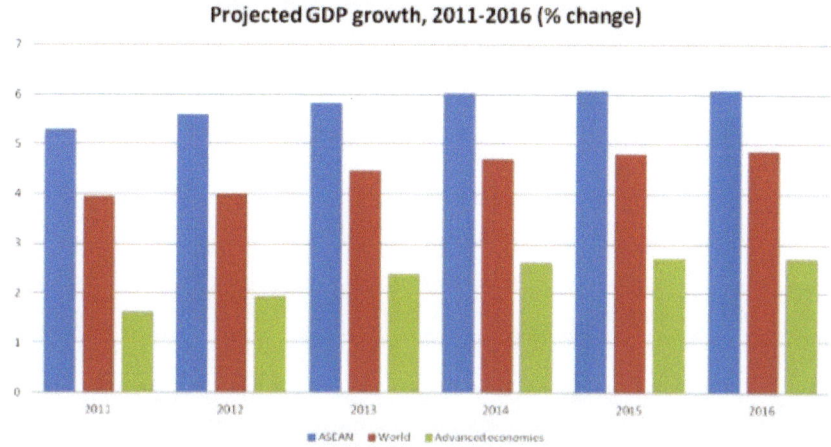

Source: International Monetary Fund, World Economic Outlook Database, September 2011

Exhibit 3: ASEAN Annual Average Growth Rate (AAGR) in percentage terms for Power Generation from Fossil Fuels (2007-2030)

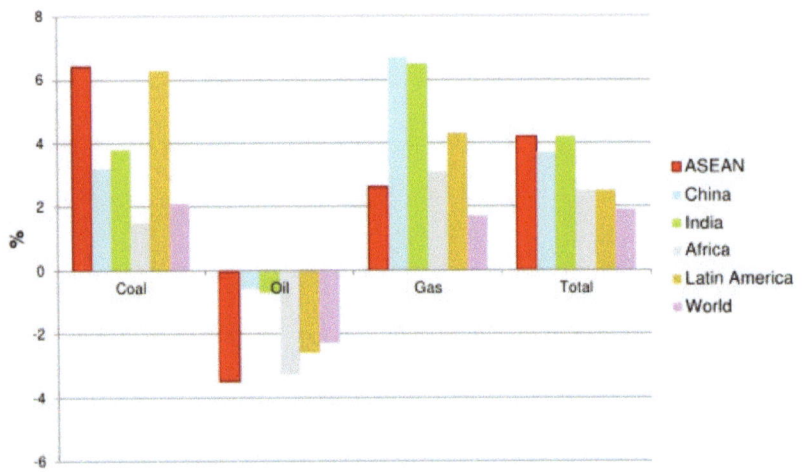

Source: IEA, World Energy Outlook 2009 (Reference Scenario)

Exhibit 4: ASEAN Annual Average Growth Rate (AAGR) in percentage terms for Power Generation from Nuclear and Renewables (2007-2030)

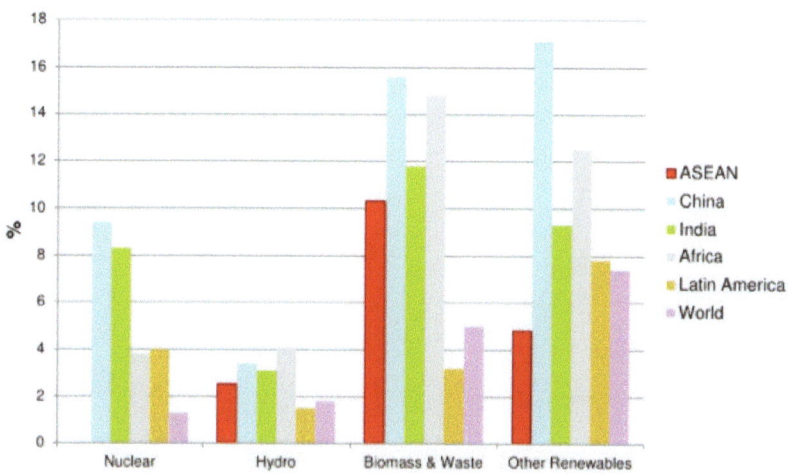

Source: IEA, World Energy Outlook 2009 (Reference Scenario)

Exhibit 5: Percentage (%) Growth in Total Final Energy Consumption by Region (2007-2030)

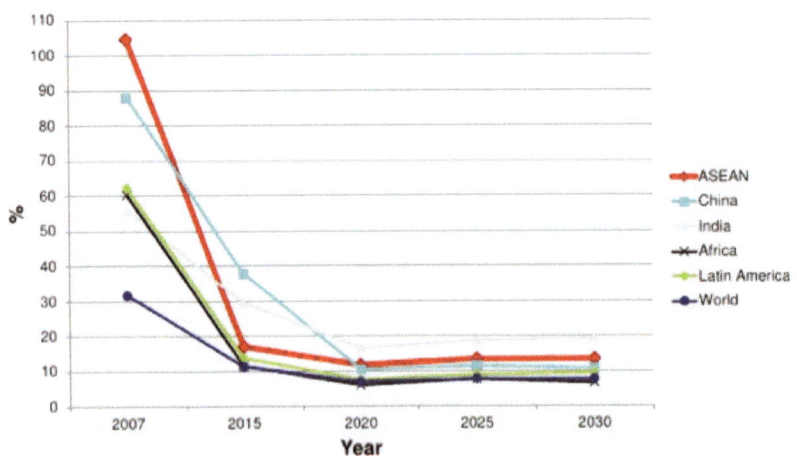

Source: IEA, World Energy Outlook 2009 (Reference Scenario)

Exhibit 6: ASEAN Power Generation (Percentage Share), 2007 and 2030 Compared, IEA Reference Scenario

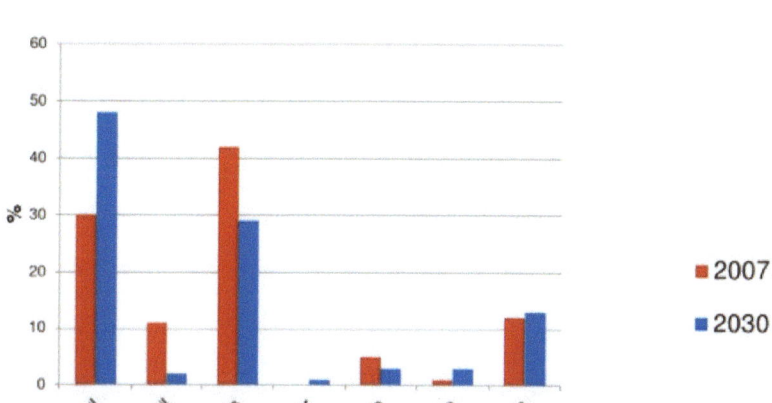

Source: IEA, World Energy Outlook 2009 (Reference Scenario)

Exhibit 7: ASEAN's Energy Resources

Fossil Energy Resources:
- **Oil** -- Brunei, Cambodia, Indonesia, Malaysia, Myanmar, Philippines, Thailand, Vietnam
- **Gas** -- Brunei, Cambodia, Indonesia, Malaysia, Myanmar, Philippines, Thailand, Vietnam
- **Coal** -- Indonesia, Malaysia, Philippines, Thailand, Vietnam

Renewable Energy Resources:
- **Hydro** -- Cambodia, Indonesia, Laos, Myanmar, Philippines, Vietnam
- **Geothermal** -- Indonesia, Philippines
- **Solar** -- all countries have various amounts
- **Wind** -- generally limited potential
- **Biomass** -- all countries have various types and amounts

Source: Energy Studies Institute

Exhibit 8: ASEAN's Projected Total Primary Energy Demand

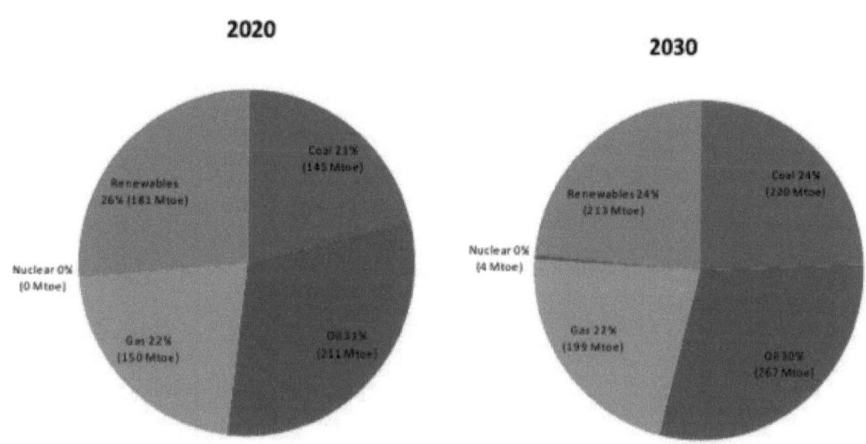

Source: IEA, World Energy Outlook 2009 (Reference Scenario)

Exhibit 9: Production, Imports and Exports of Nuclear and Renewable Energy in the ASEAN Region in 2009

Country		Nuclear and Renewable Energy Resources			
		Nuclear	Hydro	Geothermal	Biofuels & Waste
Brunei	Production	-	-	-	-
	Imports	-	-	-	-
	Exports	-	-	-	-
Cambodia	Production	-	4	-	3664
	Imports	-	-	-	-
	Exports	-	-	-	-
Indonesia	Production	-	979	15981	52981
	Imports	-	-	-	-
	Exports	-	-	-	-282
Malaysia	Production	-	574	-	3205
	Imports	-	-	-	4
	Exports	-	-	-	-223
Myanmar	Production	-	360	-	10531
	Imports	-	-	-	-
	Exports	-	-	-	-
Country		Nuclear and Renewable Energy Resources			
		Nuclear	Hydro	Geothermal	Biofuels & Waste
Philippines	Production	-	842	8881	6922
	Imports	-	-	-	33
	Exports	-	-	-	-
Singapore	Production	-	-	-	29
	Imports	-	-	-	-
	Exports	-	-	-	-
Thailand	Production	-	615	2	20538
	Imports	-	-	-	57
	Exports	-	-	-	-26
Vietnam+	Production	-	2578	-	25155
	Imports	-	-	-	-
	Exports	-	-	-	-

* Figures are thousand tones of oil equivalent. Data for Laos is unavailable.

Source: International Energy Agency, Energy Balances of Non-OECD Countries, 2011, Paris

International Energy Agency

Exhibit 10: Breakdown of ASEAN Electricity Generation in 2009 (Percentage %)

	Coal and Peat	Oil	Gas	Biofuels	Waste	Hydro	Geothermal	Solar PV	Wind
Brunei		1	99						
Cambodia		95.6		0.5		3.9			
Indonesia	41.8	22.8	22.1			7.3	6		
Malaysia	30.9	2	60.7			6.3			
Myanmar		8.9	19.6			71.5			
Philippines	26.6	8.7	32.1			15.8	16.7		0.1
Thailand	19.9	0.5	70.7	40.4		4.8	neg	neg	neg
Singapore		18.8	81		0.2				
Vietnam	18	2.5	43.4			36			

Source: International Energy Agency (IEA)

Exhibit 11: Production, Imports and Exports of Fossil Fuels in 2009

Country		Fossil Energy Resources			
		Coal and Peat	Crude Oil	Oil Products	Natural Gas
Brunei	Production	-	8485	-	10454
	Imports	-	-	98	-
	Exports	-	-7667	-	-8009
Cambodia	Production	-	-	-	-
	Imports	-	-	1473	-
	Exports	-	-	-	-
Indonesia	Production	166802	48052	-	67047
	Imports	46	18820	19458	-
	Exports	-136336	-18323	-5020	-31999
Malaysia	Production	1348	34226	-	50341
	Imports	9126	5839	7265	956
	Exports	-119	-12235	-10030	-22288
Myanmar	Production	732	1011	-	10464
	Imports	-	-	642	-
	Exports	-595	-41	-	-7215

† Figures are thousands
* Data for Laos is unavailable.

Country		Fossil Energy Resources			
		Coal and Peat	Crude Oil	Oil Products	Natural Gas
Philippines	Production	2474	1143	-	3213
	Imports	4496	6909	7440	-
	Exports	-1052	-1004	-484	-
Singapore	Production	-	-	-	-
	Imports	4	45058	89613	7093
	Exports	-	-46	-82805	-
Thailand	Production	5158	16230	-	19163
	Imports	10625	42361	448	7472
	Exports	-17	-2128	-11500	-
Vietnam	Production	24480	17330	-	7099
	Imports	465	-	14805	-
	Exports	-13995	-13614	-1811	-

† Figures are thousands
* Data for Laos is unavailable.

Source: International Energy Agency, Energy Balances of Non-OECD Countries, 2011, Paris

International Energy Agency

Exhibit 12: Energy Usage in the Transport Sector

Country	Transport Sector Energy Consumption (% of total energy consumption)
Malaysia	35.1
Philippines	35.0
Thailand	25.1
Indonesia	21.6
Singapore	20.3
Vietnam	17.3

Source: International Energy Institute, 2011

Exhibit 13: Vehicle Population of several ASEAN Countries (Indonesia, Malaysia, Singapore, Thailand, Vietnam and the Philippines) Combined till 2030

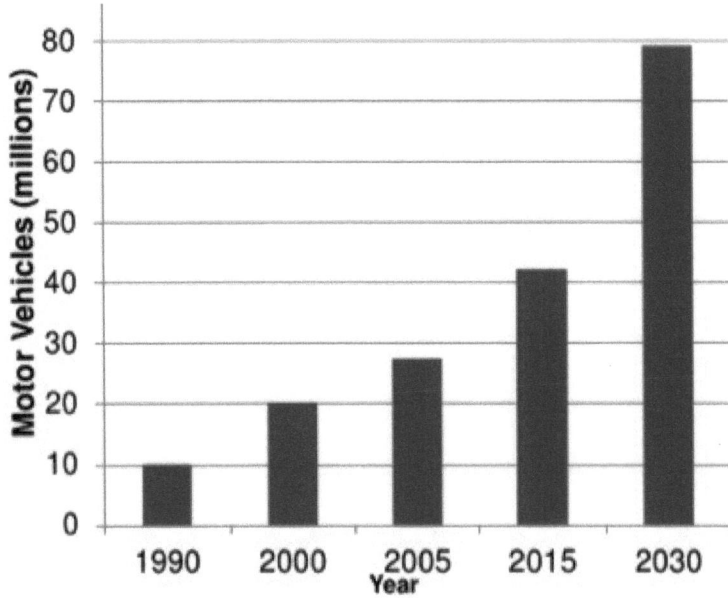

Source: Asia Pacific Energy Research Centre, APEC Energy Demand and Supply Outlook 4th Edition, 2009

Exhibit 14: Projected Transport Sector Consumption of Energy of several ASEAN Countries (Indonesia, Malaysia, Singapore, Thailand, Vietnam and the Philippines) Combined till 2030

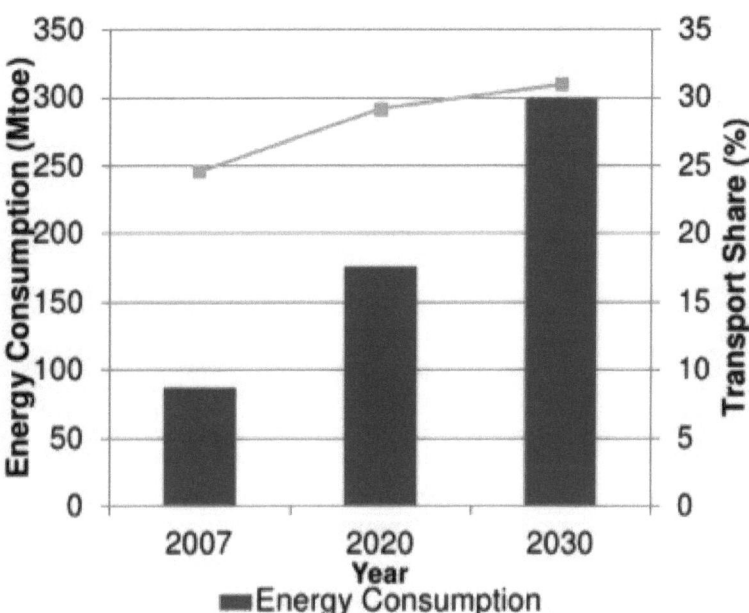

Source: Institute of Energy Economics, 3rd ASEAN Energy Outlook, Japan 2011

Exhibit 15: Vehicle Population Per Capita

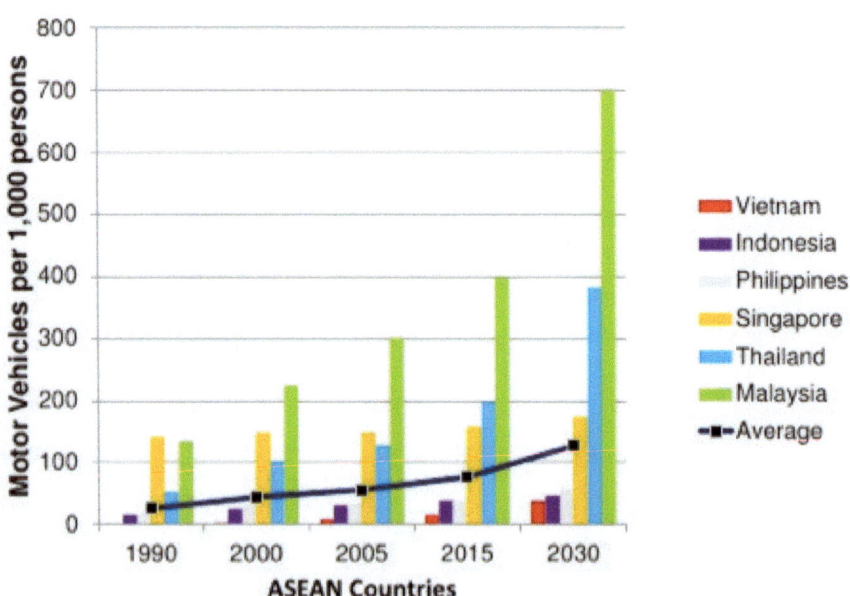

Source: APERC, APEC Energy Demand and Supply Outlook, 4th Edition

Exhibit 16: Import-Export of Petroleum Products

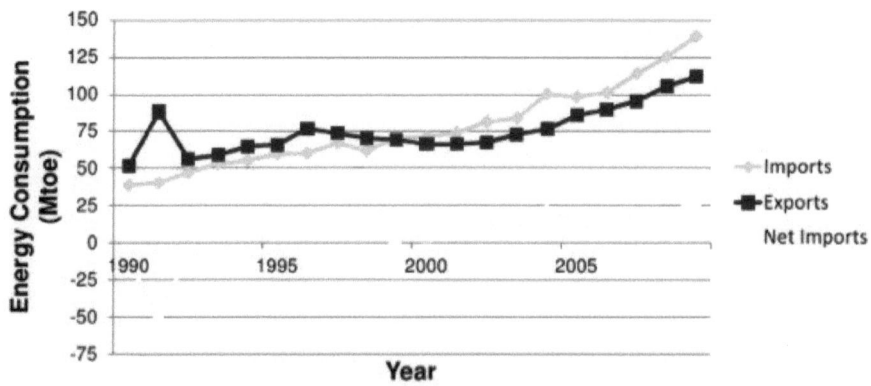

Source: International Energy Agency (IEA), 2011

Exhibit 17: ASEAN Refinery Capacities

ASEAN	Refinery Capacity (Barrels per day)
Brunei	9,000
Myanmar	57,000
Vietnam*	130,500
Philippines	282,000
Malaysia	515,000
Thailand	729,000
Indonesia	1,000,000
Singapore	1,344,000
Total	4,066,500

Source: EIA Countries Data, 2009

Exhibit 18: 2010 Pump Prices (US$ Per Litre) in ASEAN Countries

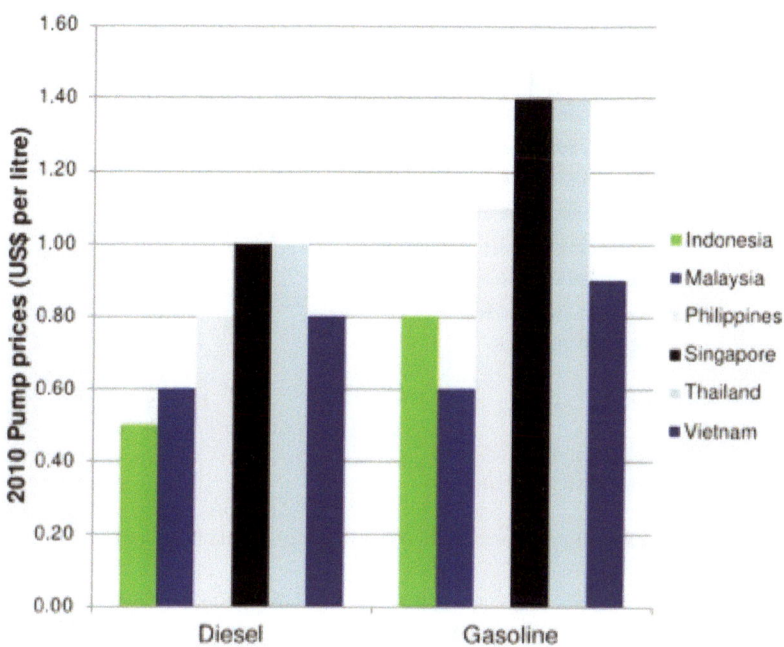

Source: World Bank, 2012

Exhibit 19: ASEAN Retail Prices of Gasoline and Diesel by Country, August 2009

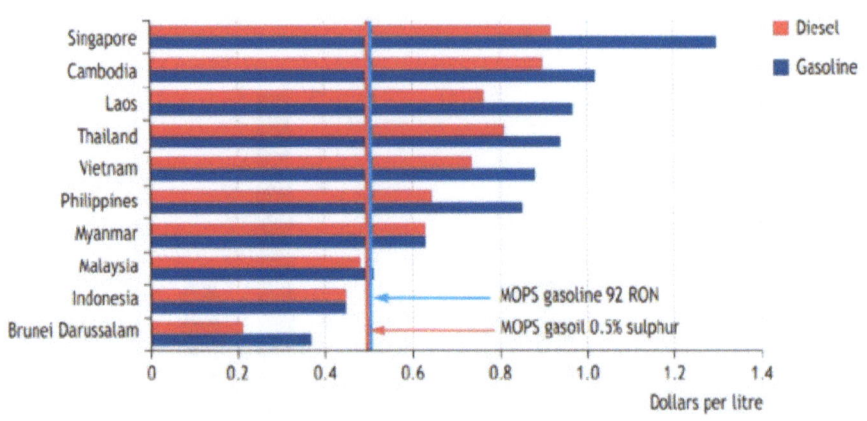

Note: MOPS in Mean of Platts Singapore

Sources: FACTS Global Energy, International Energy Agency, World Energy Outlook 2009 (Reference Scenario)

Exhibit 20: Map of the Proposed ASEAN Power Grid and Gas Pipeline Network Projects

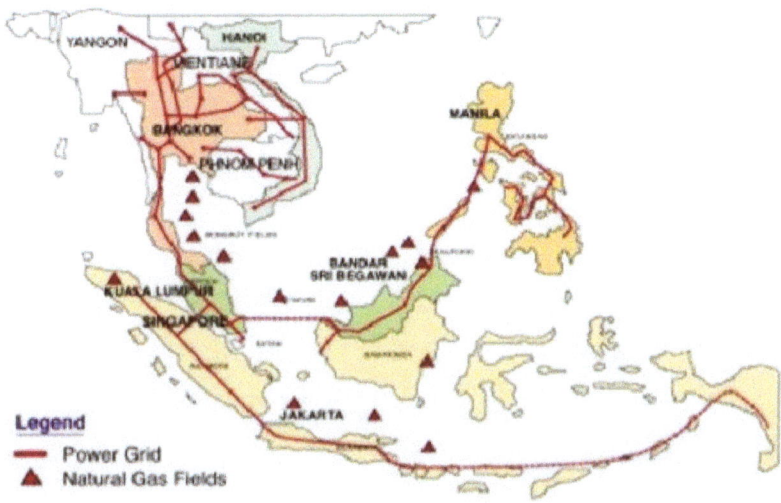

Source: Aseanenergy.org

Exhibit 21: Map of the Trans-ASEAN Gas Pipeline (TAGP)

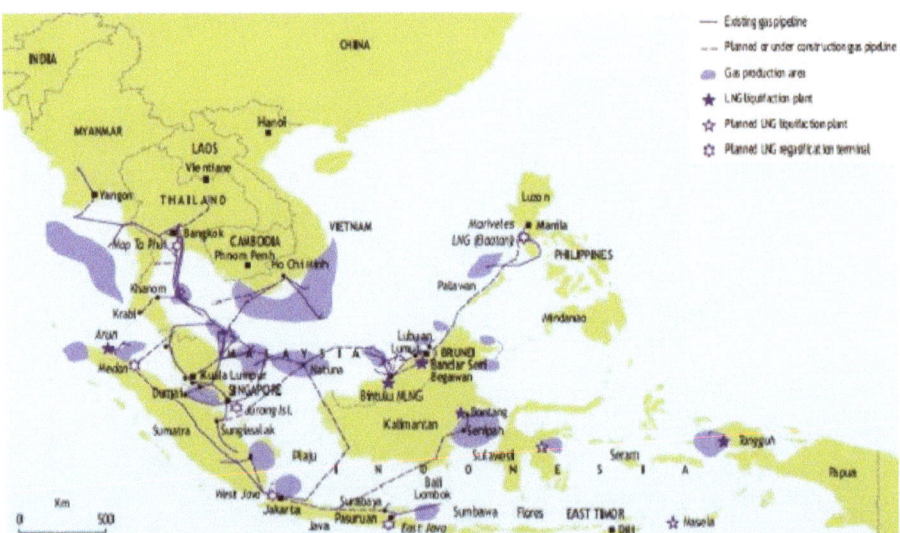

Source: ASCOPE Secretariat

Exhibit 22: Carbon and Energy Reduction Targets of Selected ASEAN, ASEAN+3 Countries

COUNTRY	REDUCTION TARGETS
CHINA	40-45% Carbon Intensity reduction by 2020 15% of energy to come from non-fossil fuels by 2020
INDONESIA	19% Carbon Emissions reduction (from energy sector) by 2020
MALAYSIA	40% Carbon Emissions reduction by 2020 (conditional, voluntary)
JAPAN	25% Carbon Emissions reduction by 2020 (1990 levels)*
SINGAPORE	35% Energy Intensity reduction by 2030 (2005 levels) 25% Carbon Intensity reduction by 2012 (1990 levels) 7-11% Carbon Emissions reduction by 2020 (BAU levels, unconditional) 16% Carbon Emissions reduction by 2020 (BAU, conditional)
S. KOREA	30% Carbon Emissions reduction (forecast levels)
THAILAND	30% Carbon Emissions reductions (from energy sector) by 2020
VIETNAM	5% of electricity to come from non-fossil fuels by 2020

Source: Energy Studies Institute

Exhibit 23: Strong Renewable Energy Potential at Selected ASEAN Countries

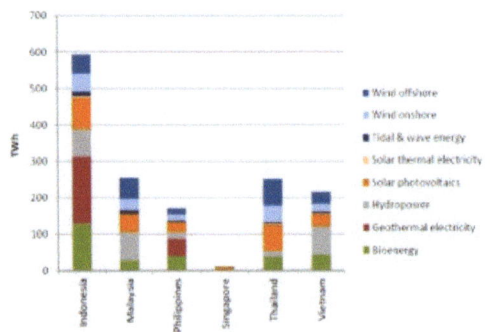
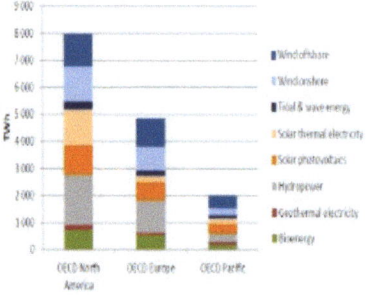

2030 Renewable Electricity Potentials in ASEAN-6 Countries (source: IEA 2011)

2030 Renewable Electricity Potentials in Major OECD-30 Sub-regions (source: IEA 2011)

Source: International Energy Agency (IEA), 2011

Exhibit 24: Poor Energy Efficiency in ASEAN

Country	(billion kWh)	Losses as % of total net generation
Brunei	0.218	6%
Burma (Myanmar)	0.22	34%
Cambodia	15.36	19%
Indonesia	0.26	10%
Laos	3.99	7%
Malaysia	1.91	4%
Philippines	7.5	13%
Singapore	2.16	5%
Thailand	8.78	6%
Vietnam	7.99	10%
China	181.15	5%
United States	260.58	7%
India	219.87	6%
OECD	662.78	7%

Source: Energy Studies Institute

Exhibit 25: Key Energy Challenges in Each Country

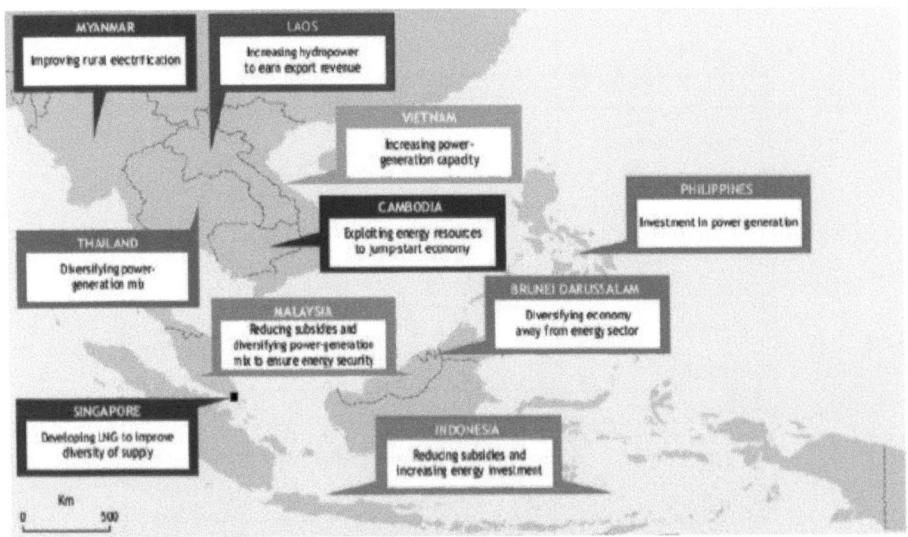

Source: International Energy Agency, World Energy Outlook 2009 (Reference Scenario)

Exhibit 26: Major Programmes and Targets for Improving Access to Electricity in ASEAN

Country	Program Name	Description	Financing Arrangements
Cambodia	Renewable Energy Strategy	- all villages to have electricity by 2020 - 70% of all rural households to be electrified by 2030 - Remaining 30% of rural households will be targeted through the Renewable Energy Development Programme.	Data unavailable
Indonesia	Rural Electrification Programme – National Energy Management	- 90% electrification for 2020.	Cross subsidies by state owned power utility (PNL) and donors
Lao PDR	Rural Electrification Programme	-80% households to be electrified by 2015. - 90% households to be electrified by 2020. -Electrification of 42,000 rural households through connection to grid of Electricité du Laos (EdL) - Phase 2 will further provide electrification to 10,000 households through off-grid technologies	Cross subsidies and foreign investors (decentralized solutions)
Philippines	Philippines Energy Plan (2004-2013)	- 90% of households to be electrified by 2017.	Grants and loans from a National Electrification Fund and public-private partnerships.

Source: International Energy Agency, World Energy Outlook 2011

About The Author

Dr. Tan Kwan Hong serves as professor for finance, economics, business, leadership and human resource management. Beyond his involvement as a professor, lecturer and an academic writer, he is also an award-winning corporate trainer and lecturer and has given talks to more than 120,000 people on topics such as leadership, entrepreneurship, management skills, communication skills, persuasion, career management skills and personal peak performance.

Apart from accomplishing his Doctor of Philosophy, Dr. Tan Kwan Hong has 3 Masters degrees, in particular, the Master of Science (Finance) (With Distinction) from Grenoble Ecole de Management, the Master of Science (Human Resource) (With Distinction) from Edinburgh Napier University, and the Master of Education (With High Distinction) from Monash University.

He has also obtained 3 graduate diplomas to supplement his knowledge, in particular, the Specialist Diploma in Business Analytics (With Merit) from Temasek Polytechnic, the Post Graduate Diploma in Business Administration (With High Distinction) and the Graduate Diploma in Training and Development (With High Distinction), both from Aventis School of Management in Singapore. He has scored in the top grade category for all Masters and Graduate Diploma programs, and was the overall top student for several of these programs.

Dr. Tan Kwan Hong first graduated from the Singapore Management University with the Bachelor of Science (Economics) (With Distinction).

As an avid learner, Dr. Tan Kwan Hong has also obtained more than 150 different certifications in the areas of business analytics, finance, human resource, project management and sports science. He is a Certified Business Analytics Specialist (CBAS) and a Certified Associate in Project Management (CAPM). He is also a Distinguished

Toastmasters (DTM), the highest accolade achievable from Toastmasters International, only awarded to less than 1% of all members worldwide.

As a national science champion in his youth, Dr. Tan Kwan Hong was also the recipient of several scholarships, academic and university awards, national awards, public speaking awards, and also has a national-level strategy case competition championship title. He has also represented his country in regional conferences on academic and policy issues.

Dr. Tan Kwan Hong's corporate experience spans strategy consulting, financial research, education management and policy development. He can be contacted at www.tankwanhong.com and www.linkedin.com/in/tankwanhong.